Fathers aren't Mothers

Saanle Hebert

Saanle Hebert

TABLE OF CONTENT

CONCLUSION

Fathers aren't Mothers

INTRODUCTION

With regards to raising girls, mothers regularly get the greater part of the tension and the credit. Whether with respect to feminine issues, kid issues, or cosmetics tips, mother is generally the principal individual every daughter goes to. This side-covering of fathers is predominant in mainstream society also - numerous famous Television programs frequently depict fathers as blundering bozos with regards to "girls stuff." All of this can leave fathers feeling underestimated or powerless and, far more atrocious; can keep daughters from getting every one of the advantages of a tight bond with their fathers. Fathers aren't mothers, this is valid, and for that reason little girls need them.

Fathers aren't Mothers

CHAPTER ONE

Fathers Aren't Mothers

A great deal has changed for fathers over the beyond couple of ages, says Gary Brown, Ph.D., an authorized marriage and family specialist in Los Angeles. "75 years prior, fathers weren't permitted in the conveyance room; presently, fathers are there all along," he says. "Fathers today are considerably more educated and associated with their kids, taking a functioning part in the sustaining of their kids, from taking care of whether communicated bosom milk or equation to evolving diapers, relieving, clothing, washing, perusing to, and assisting their child with falling asleep." This nurturing change in outlook has prompted critical advantages for the two fathers and little girls, he says. By being a fundamental piece of these early years, fathers have the chance to shape a critical security with their newborn child little girls, making a sound between reliance and assisting their girls with remembering them as a steady wellspring of supporting, wellbeing, insurance, regard, and love. This gives a protected base from which a young lady figures out how to investigate the world and connect with others.

As girls age into the school years, fathers become significantly more vital to their physical, mental, and social wellbeing. "It would be hard to exaggerate the strong impact that fathers have in the molding of their girls' perspectives about their own mental self portrait, values, sexuality, connections, and their entitlement to decide the course of their own lives," Dr. Brown makes sense of. Young girls who have a warm, good relationship with their fathers are better ready to deal with ordinary stressors, are less inclined to wretchedness and tension, and are better ready to discuss their sentiments, as per a review distributed in the Diary of Family Brain science. Furthermore, young ladies with involved fathers are likewise undeniably less inclined to go hungry, to live in neediness, and to have better actual wellbeing, as per a subsequent report done by Rutgers.

Because of a fast increment of sex chemicals and the little girl's developing requirement for individuation, the teenager years can be an abnormal time in the father-daughter relationship. However, Dr. Brown, According to earthy colored, daughters need their fathers like never before during this period of improvement. As a matter of fact, depending on their personality, young ladies might feel more open to conversing with their fathers than to their mothers about specific touchy issues. For example, they might favor a male viewpoint on dating or they might have the option to be more open with their fathers. For this reason fathers need to oppose the compulsion to see their girls as the small kid they used to be and on second thought utilize this chance to assemble a more grounded relationship with the lady she's becoming. Fathers play a critical role during this transition from teen to youthful grown-up, as indicated by a new report distributed in the Diary of North American Brain research. Daughters who detailed having mindful, involved fathers had higher confidence and more noteworthy generally speaking life fulfillment than their companions who had more wild connections - and that lift endured well into school. Likewise, a review distributed in the Diary of Contemporary Brain science, observed that fathers might assume a part in if Daughters foster dietary problems during this period.

As little girls develop into youthful grown-ups and start to look for autonomy from their families, fathers actually play a significant part. However, it will end up being a more warning one, Dr. Earthy colored says. While this can be difficult for adoring fathers, it's a fundamental and significant piece of their little girls' turn of events. "By establishing that relationship of trust early not right off the bat, young ladies will feel open to coming to their dads for exhortation about connections, vocations, and life," he says. However, regardless of the vast advantages for both father and girl, numerous men pass up this significant relationship - halfway from dread and incompletely from an off track feeling of what's legitimate in light of obsolete generalizations. "I see too many men buy into the idea of 'that is a girl's issue' or 'just a lady can get another lady' and abstain from conversing with their girls about sex, dating, or other 'silly' points. They might accept their girls ought to consequently squeeze into biased orientation jobs," Dr. Earthy colored says. "I likewise see men who are gotten into their own limited perspective on being a dad to their little girl. They accept that their main job is as a supplier and defender, and they wind up working excessively and passing up those brilliant dad little girl holding minutes. It doesn't need to be that way by any stretch of the imagination."

See yourself in that portrayal? Try not to thrash yourself. No parent is great, yet putting forth the attempt to have a decent relationship can yield compensate that endure forever for both father and little girl, Dr. Earthy colored says.

The Facts on Fathers

Research affirms, over and over, that a Father assumes a one-of-a-kind part in the advancement of his daughters' confidence, conduct, life decisions, and connections. "Higher levels of father involvement in activities with their children, such as eating, suppers together, going on trips, and assisting with schoolwork, are related with fewer conduct issues, more elevated levels of amiability, and a more significant level of school execution among kids and youths. With regards to the particular father-daughter relationship, Father's inclusion is interestingly compelling. ""Fathers have an incalculable impact on their daughters," composes Dr. James Dobson in the Total Marriage and Family Home Reference Guide." Most psychologists believe that all future close connections to happen in a girls life will be affected emphatically or adversely by the way in which she sees and cooperates with her father.

In the event that he dismisses and disregards her, she will go through her time on earth attempting to supplant him in her heart. Assuming he is warm and sustaining, she will search for a sweetheart to approach him. Assuming he thinks she is delightful, commendable, and female, she will be leaned to view herself as such." All things being equal, a father has the chance to show his girl how a genuine man treats a lady, setting the norm for her future associations with men.

Gary Thomas says, "When my girls were growing up, I attempted to set the bar as high as could be expected - I needed to attest them, support them and even ruin them a bit, so a person would need to do likewise to raise in her as a possible mate. Assuming a person at any point got unpleasant with them, or put them down, they'd think, that is not the way in which solid men treat ladies."

At last, Thomas says, a daughter's relationship with her father fundamentally affects her perspective on men, her perspective on God, and her perspective on herself.

Reasons Fathers Connect Better With Daughters

Fathers have a novel bond with their girls and it's very unique in relation to the bond they share with their children. While the mother-child bond is greatly recognized, investigated, and straightforwardly discussed, the relationship of a father with his girl has not been given as much concentration. Many think that a father's job is critical in trimming a little child into a grown-up, yet much neglect to completely comprehend the impacts fathers have on their girls. Therapists have been underscoring the mother-child bond as the essential impact on the kid's personality - up to this point. Studies have been directed appearance that the father affects his daughters more than a mother with regards to deeply shaping their way of behaving.

Studies have also shown that girls who have a superior relationship with their fathers will quite often enjoy numerous individual benefits, for example, better heartfelt connections, better conduct qualities, helped confidence, good self-perception, great independence, and better dynamic capacities. Then again, the shortfall of a mentor or a sincerely far off father has been referred to as one of the most widely recognized factors for a girl to grow up thoughtful, maintain biased viewpoints of the other gender, settle on imprudent choices, and take part in temperamental connections, all, while she turns moderately more disastrous as she attempts to adapt to this, need her life.

He Is the First Man in Her Life

A father is the main man a young lady experiences in her day-to-day existence. Her thoughts regarding the contrary orientation are formed into being by noticing him. Her perspectives on men are an immediate result of her relationship with him, how he tends to himself, and how he acts with her mom. A caring father ingrain in her an inspirational perspective on men, causes her to feel sure, ready to cherish and trust, focus on committed relationships, and adds to her psychological, enthusiastic, physical, and otherworldly wellbeing. On the other hand, a far-off father who continually contends and affronts her mom drives her to expect that all men are something similar - impolite and legitimate. She effectively gets connected to her father as she realizes what a man may be and finds in him what a man should be.

Studies have shown that young ladies perpetually wanted that their associations with their fathers were genuinely and by and by closer. They accepted that with a nearer relationship, they could serenely discuss private matters, for example, marriage and separation, medication and liquor use, monetary issues, wretchedness, dietary issues, and sex before marriage

He Is Her Protector

Generally, a man's sense is to secure. Men by and large have more actual strength so the orientation jobs have been with the end goal that a man is looked for assurance and an individual for care. This reels back to the 'made in trouble's subject we so generally experience in folklore, expressions, and music since days of yore. An early model is the narrative of the legend, Peruses, saving youthful lady Andromeda, who was affixed to a stone by the ocean, by killing a monster released ashore by the Greek god Poseidon. For what reason are girls joined to their fathers? A dad ordinarily sees his better half and girls to be needing assurance and security, and he should give that to them. This is likewise the justification for why fathers are by and large saw as critical and uncertain about young men their girl's date; they know how men think, and can incidentally distinguish the horrendous men from the great ones.

His Daughter Is More Affectionate

Sons are frequently instructed to be more in charge of their feelings. This can be ascribed to normal practices, notwithstanding his own father censuring him to turn into an all the more genuinely changed man and not a "sissy." This causes them to subdue their feelings, which doesn't actually help in holding with the father. Since little girls will generally be more expressive than children, they are generally anxious to show their love with basic motions and articulations - the best being her grin. For an all-father day and gets back home all exhausted, a major ear-to-ear grin with a little sparkle in the eye from his girl makes every one of the dissatisfactions, work and work worth the effort. Most fathers additionally see their little girls as the ones who will deal with them as they become older while expecting that the sons will neglect them for their spouses once they wed.

Saanle Hebert

He Cares For His Daughter as Much, If Not More

While it's undeniably true that fathers assume a gigantic part in the person trim of young men, their impact on young ladies isn't tremendously perceived. As entertainer Ryan Reynolds once said, fathers will 'stroll through a concrete divider to get to her.' Studies have demonstrated fathers to be sterner in a kid's childhood, bringing about the kid recognizing his dad principally as a good example and conduct shaper, however considerably less as somebody with a passionate association. Conversely, young ladies partake in a more permissive methodology from their dads, and are regularly blamed for 'folding him over her little finger.' Something beyond differential treatment, this tolerance can be ascribed to cultural standards where a young lady is imparted with enthusiastic expressivity and delicacy, and the kid is educated to stifle such sentiments that are thought of "ladylike." The normal origination, then, is that a father's obligation is to make his children extreme while he sees his girls as delicate and needing security; thusly, he shows his minding in a more passionate manner with his little girl.

A Daughter Is More Compassionate

Passionate ability is regularly considered a lady's comparable to a man's actual strength. Ladies might be more effectively wounded by passionate encounters than men, yet they can beat it in a more limited timeframe. As ladies are by and large more sincerely responsive, they assimilate in themselves the capacity to pay attention to other people and offer in their pain. Little girls do precisely that, by bringing out the stifled enthusiastic side of a man. Fathers, particularly single parents, are normally more open about their concerns when a girl is around in light of the fact that he tracks down her more understanding of his choices and decisions; she is less critical than her male siblings. This again returns to the differential childhood hypothesis referenced before where young men are raised to be intense and young ladies as delicate and adoring. This adds to the dad's more grounded bond with his girl as she crosses her adolescent years and turns out to be more developed.

A Daughter Can Be More Obedient

Fathers trust girls to be more focused and devoted than their children. There is substantially less rubbing between a father and his girl principally in light of the fact that young ladies admire their dads as awesome of men, and soak up in themselves every one of the perspectives and assessments the father holds as obvious. This can again be made sense of how different societies and social orders force on her they should be sensitive and cultured, which converts into her turning out to be more respectful sometime down the road - yet this may not generally essentially be the situation. Studies have shown that a young lady will in general accidentally favor her father's desire for music, proficient courses, governmental issues, and even will in general hold his perspective on religion and otherworldliness. Her dad resembles a mirror to the rest of the world, and all that she sees is colored by what she gains from him during her adolescence. This reflection is a lift to his self-image, making him more attracted to his daughter. This makes fathers normally incline toward their girls and show them more fondness.

The Age Factor

Age influences the manner in which a little girl bonds with her parents; different matured young ladies bond diversely with every one of their parents. While the boys might have a consistent relationship with his parents all through his life, a young lady's relationship will in general continue changing and advancing, inclining toward one parent over the other. At first, since the mother is distinguished as the essential guardian, the young lady fosters a more profound relationship with her. As she becomes older, she starts to distinguish her father as the supplier and despises her mom's connection to him, in the long run seeing her as contest to accumulate her father's friendship. She grows new needs that are satisfied by the dad, making her approval him more. As she arrives at pubescence, she briefly removes herself from her dad and looks for her mom to direct her through this time of progress. Once more once she is composed to this change, the bond with her dad is fixed, and she looks for his recommendation on choices, relationships and life overall.

Family Dynamics Influence Her

The environment around her - how her kin view their parents, how her mom sees her father - makes an imprint on a young lady and impacts how she interfaces with him. Fathers who over and again misuse their spouses before the kids have the most far-off bond with their children, and this is, in all reasonableness, their own doing. With regards to favoring one side, regardless of whether girls bond better with the father, generally, the mother is picked by the kid in such circumstances. She sees her own appearance in her mom, and such situations make her figure that her father doesn't adore her. Kin additionally impacts a young lady's relationship; a young lady who has a dad and a sibling in her family has her warm gestures split between every one of them. Her sibling acquires greater conspicuousness in her life, to such an extent that assuming he hates their father, she detests him, and assuming he praises her father, she also does likewise.

There Is No Competition between Them

In the survey led by Netmums, moms portrayed their boys in certain words, for example, 'amusing,' 'brassy,' 'adoring' and 'perky,' though their little girls were depicted on a fairly basic note with words, for example, 'genuine' and 'contentious.' While boys admire their fathers, they are additionally in a never-ending rivalry with their fathers to be the "extremely confident man" of the family. Likewise, girls have a sensation of inadequacy contrasted with their mothers concerning looks, mind, character, or conduct, and hence endeavor to be preferable over them. Different investigations have recommended that girls consider their mom to be a contest and, somewhat, there is an inner self-conflict between them. Along these lines, the girl decides to imitate her mom's dressing style, her character, even her perspective, to show up better according to herself as well as other people. In any case, it's a totally inverse response with the dad. A long way from being cutthroat, fathers will more often than not sincerely affect little girls, which helps construct their personality and dynamic capacities sometime down the road. Father will cause her to feel pretty and unique, and for this reason, they share a more grounded bond.

Fathers aren't Mothers

CHAPTER TWO

How to Build a Strong Father Daughter Bond

The manner in which a daughter sees her father will be the manner in which she sees men sometime down the road. In any event, when they're a distant memory, that mentor will wait on and show up in a wide range of parts of a daughter's life. She will raise her children as her father raised her, and move that shrewdness she gained from her dad onto people in the future. On the off chance that a father can furnish their little girl with security, while as yet empowering her to develop further lady, she will actually want to trust men and foster solid connections later on. A dad's presence has as quite a bit of an impact as the absence of such a presence - a job seemly affects an individual regardless of whether they choose to play it. Those illustrations are on the whole being conveyed not by everything a father says to his little girl, but rather by how he communicates with her and her mom. While a mother can fill in as a good example, a dad will show her what's in store of different men.

Knowing all the impacts of a strong father-daughter bond, how do we achieve it?

All father-daughter bonds will be unique. Everyone is unique and valuable on its own particular manner. Everyone gains something else from their daddy at various times. In any case, there are a few key components that ought to be investigated while shaping a solid and adoring father- daughter bond.

Be Present from the Start

All new parents feel overpowered from the get-go. With no preparation or accreditation, you've been given control of another human existence. At the point when you discover that you're having a girl, you can support that bond quickly by basically being available. Your accomplice will endure the worst part of a portion of the consideration, however, be available to relieve your infant girl, change her nappy, give her a shower, rock her while mum showers. By putting forth the attempt to be available for your girl, even in those early days, you will lastingly affect her life.

Quality Time

Fathers should be there, and not exactly when challenges are out of hand. Being available is stage one in shaping a solid bond. There will continuously be pardons that might have you around short of what you could be, work or life balance. There will continuously feel like some other opportunity to make it dependent upon them however when your girl actually needs you is at this moment. Set forth the energy. Your little girl will thank you for it in years to come.

Play Together

Play a game around the house. Anything it is be there to give your little girl an essential close friend. Whenever you play with your girl, she considers you to be her essential close friend and has the chance to feel like the focal point of consideration. Assuming you invest in some opportunity to show her the principles of a game, for instance, you can expand on that relationship by taking more time to a game to see it live and empowering her to engage in that specific action herself. In the event that sports aren't her thing attempt workmanship or shading? An action like this is a great method for holding regardless of whether you both aren't maturing specialists; you can in any case enjoy a ton of chuckles. Drawing is something you can really figure out how to improve at, so both of you can gain ground together and develop while you extend your relationship.

Emotional Support

There's a period when most dads put a solid boundary in their associations with their little girls and that is the basic teenager time frame when they begin developing into ladies. You want to comprehend that this is a mistaking period for them to the truth of the matter is that your childhood had various stages and you can never completely understand what she's going through, however that doesn't mean you shouldn't give your all to attempt.

Listen to Her

As above, when she is going through this stage, it could be extreme for you to comprehend or know how to help her. Listen is your best instrument here. Pay attention to her when she is letting you know something. Try not to pass judgment on her or become furious. She wants to learn she can believe you and that together you can sort out anything. Regardless of anything else, you would rather not miss your girl turning into an adult since that precise period is the point at which she will foster solid qualities that will later be a piece of her character. Normally, this is the point at which she really wants your assistance most, regardless of whether she understands it, so show up for her. It may not generally go without a hitch - odds are good that they will not - however, your work will not be inconspicuous.

CHAPTER THREE

CONCLUSION

Everybody has different relationship with their parents; however the most perfect bond that one will find is of father to daughter.. A father shields her daughter from each thing which is terrible for her, he will in general make her daughter the prettiest and the most stickler on the planet. Daughters genuinely must have great connection with their father, as it impacts their character, their prosperity, their way of behaving. Daughters who have a decent connection with their dads are adequately fortunate to glance back at their affectionate recollections when they grow up. Having a decent connection with fathers shapes a daughters youth experience as well as impacts her way of behaving towards different men further down the road. On the off chance that a daughter-father is flighty or totally missing commonly, it makes a sensation of low confidence in her, and she could experience difficulty confiding in men overall. A daughter- father go about as a legend for her , this is on the grounds that he is the principal man she is acquainted with , he is the primary man who holds her, her discernment about a man is fostered the manner in which her father treats her. This insight is significant for a young girls' development.

Father's presences not just coordinates daughter in the beginning phase of life yet in addition guarantee her that whatever the issue is her father is remaining as an ice sheet before her and will safeguard her from each issue.